Margret Beran

Ich versteh nur Bahnhof!

500 Redewendungen
für den Alltag

Deutsch – Englisch

Hueber Verlag

3.	2.	1.		Die letzten Ziffern
2014	13	12	11	10	bezeichnen Zahl und Jahr des Druckes.

Alle Drucke dieser Auflage können, da unverändert, nebeneinander benutzt werden.
1. Auflage
© 2010 Hueber Verlag, 85737 Ismaning, Deutschland
Umschlaggestaltung: Parzhuber und Partner, München
Zeichnungen: Martin Guhl, Stein am Rhein, Schweiz
Layout: Sarah-Vanessa Schäfer, Hueber Verlag, Ismaning
Satz: Satz+Layout Fruth GmbH, München
Druck und Bindung: Ludwig Auer GmbH, Donauwörth
Printed in Germany
ISBN 978–3–19–107892–8

Vorwort

Das Lernen einer fremden Sprache wird mit dem Öffnen eines Fensters zur Welt verglichen. In der Tat merkt man bald, dass mit dem Wort Erfahrungen, Bilder und Denkweisen transportiert werden, die nicht unbedingt mit denen des eigenen Landes übereinstimmen müssen. Früher oder später gelangt man dann an den Punkt, wo man zwar den ungefähren Sinn eigener Äußerungen in der Fremdsprache wiedergeben kann, das aber doch unbefriedigend bleibt, da man den „Nagel nicht auf den Kopf zu treffen" vermag, weil in der eigenen Sprache kein „neutraler" Ausdruck, sondern eine Redensart verwendet wird.

Redensarten lassen aus Wörtern etwas Lebendiges entstehen und geben dem Ausdruck Farbe. Allerdings sind sie es auch, die uns leicht in die Irre führen. Ähnlich lautende Idiome und Redensarten können in der fremden Sprache einen anderen Sinn haben, bedeutungsverschoben sein, oder sie existieren in einem völlig anderen Bild. So ist beispielsweise „auf den Busch klopfen" im Englischen keineswegs *to beat about the bush*; während die Deutschen „Eulen nach Athen tragen", bedeutet dies für den Engländer *to carry coals to Newcastle*.

Auch kann es vorkommen, dass in der anderen Sprache gar kein idiomatisches Äquivalent existiert, der Gebrauch der Redensart auf einen bestimmten Kontext eingeschränkt ist oder man aus mehreren Varianten die treffendste auswählen muss.
Die meisten Ausdrücke können nicht stilistisch indifferent verwendet werden, sie sind häufig recht salopp und gehören in die Umgangssprache. Darum sollte man vorsichtig mit dem Gebrauch sein, denn Redewendungen können leicht falsch oder unangemessen verwendet werden.

Die vorliegende Sammlung deutscher Redensarten einschließlich bildhafter Einzelworte mit ihren englischen Entsprechungen soll helfen, Missverständnisse im Sprachgebrauch zu vermeiden. Es werden Vorschläge gemacht, wie gebräuchliche deutsche Redewendungen im Englischen möglichst sinngemäß und mit der nötigen stilistischen Färbung verwendet werden können. Dabei wird davon ausgegangen, dass der Benutzer die deutsche Sprache und deren unterschiedliche stilistische Ebenen sicher beherrscht.

Als Ordnungsprinzip wurde das erste Substantiv der Wendung bzw. ein Hauptstichwort gewählt.

Die Wiedergabe deutscher Redensarten und idiomatischer Wendungen bezieht sich auf das britische Englisch.

Während Sprichwörter (prov) auch im Deutschen gekennzeichnet sind, werden stilistische Einschränkungen nur für das Englische angegeben.

Folgende linguistische Abkürzungen werden verwendet:

(A.E.)   amerikanisches Englisch
(coll)   umgangssprachlich
(vulg)   vulgär
(dated)   veraltet
(bibl)   biblischen Ursprungs
(franz)   französisch
FF   *false friend*

Die beiliegende MP3-CD enthält alle Redewendungen, Übersetzungen und Beispielsätze aus dem Buch.

Anmerkung:

Leider stößt man immer wieder auf gebräuchliche deutsche Redewendungen, die nur mit einer direkten Übersetzung ins Englische übertragen werden könnten, aber dort keinen Sinn machen. Hier seien nur einige genannt: Undank ist der Welt Lohn. Mal den Teufel nicht an die Wand! Höflichkeit ist eine Zier ... Bei Nacht sind alle Katzen grau. Humor ist, wenn man trotzdem lacht. Aller guten Dinge sind drei. Man soll die Feste feiern, wie sie fallen. Was sich liebt, das neckt sich. Scherben bringen Glück. Ein Kuckucksei ins Nest legen. Eine Schnapszahl.

Margret Beran

Inhaltsverzeichnis

Track 1

A • von A bis Z
from A to Z (coll), from start to finish
▶ He will have no difficulty explaining what has happened because he knows the whole story from A to Z.

A • das A und O
the be-all and end-all, the essence
▶ Flexibility and politeness are the be-all and end-all of my present job.

aalglatt • aalglatt sein
to be as slippery as an eel (coll)
▶ He can't be pinned down on any of these crimes. He is as slippery as an eel.

abgebrannt • abgebrannt sein
to be (flat) broke (coll), to be skint (coll), to be stony broke (dated) (coll), not to have a bean (dated) (coll)
▶ I can't lend you anything – I'm flat broke.

abgebrüht • abgebrüht sein
to be a tough cookie (coll), to be thick-skinned (coll)
▶ He is a very tough cookie. When I told him about his sister's death, he didn't react at all.

abnehmen • Das nehme ich dir nicht ab!
You're (You've got to be) kidding! (coll) / Pull the other one! (coll) / You're having me on! (coll)

Abreibung • eine Abreibung bekommen
to get a good hiding (coll), to get a good thrashing (coll)
▶ The boy got a good hiding from his angry father.

absahnen

to cash in (on sth) (coll), to rake it in (coll), to make a pretty penny (out of sth) (coll)
▶ Car manufacturers have been able to cash in on inadequate public transport systems.

abschminken • Das kannst du dir abschminken!

to forget sth (coll), to put sth out of one's mind (coll), to write sth off
▶ You can forget that idea.
▶ You can put that idea right out of your mind.

Abstellgleis • aufs Abstellgleis geschoben werden

to put sbd in a backwater (coll)
▶ After his successes in America the boss put him in a backwater for fear of being overtaken by him.

Achse • ständig auf Achse sein

to be always on the move
▶ Ever since he got that new job he has been constantly on the move, one week in London, one week in Rome.

Track 2

ad • ad acta legen

to shelve sth (coll)
▶ Let's shelve the question since we won't be able to solve the problem anyway.

Ader • eine Ader für etwas haben

to be a gifted ..., to be a born ...
▶ He is a gifted musician. / He is a born musician.

Adresse • an die falsche Adresse kommen
to knock at the wrong door, to bark up the wrong tree (coll)
▶ He asked Simon to vote for the Radical Party, but he was knocking at the wrong door – Simon's very conservative.

Affäre • sich aus der Affäre ziehen
to wriggle out of sth (coll), to get out of sth, to extricate oneself from sth
▶ The Government has been trying to wriggle out of the mess for months, but nobody believes that it was not involved.

Affe • einen Affen haben
(Redewendungen, geordnet nach zunehmendem Grad von Betrunkenheit)
to be tipsy, to have had a few (coll), to be oiled (coll), to be lubricated (coll), to be plastered (coll), to be smashed (coll), to be pissed (vulg), to be legless (coll)
▶ The football team went to the pub after the match and they all got completely smashed.

Altenteil • sich aufs Altenteil setzen / zurückziehen
to be put out to grass (coll); to retire
▶ After working for forty-five years he was put out to grass.

Amtsschimmel • Da wiehert der Amtschimmel!
red tape
▶ We are getting buried in red tape!

anbaggern • jmd anbaggern
to pick up (coll), to get off with (coll) (stärker, normalerweise mit sexuellen Folgen)
▶ He picks up a different girl every other week, but I don't know if he ever really gets off with them.

Anblick • kein erfreulicher Anblick sein
to be a sorry sight
▶ The new playground is a sorry sight – almost everything has already been vandalized.

andrehen • jmd etwas andrehen
to fob sth off on sbd, to palm sth off on sbd (coll)
▶ Someone had tried to fob her off with a forged ten pound note.

Track 3

Angelegenheiten • sich um seine eigenen Angelegenheiten kümmern
to mind one's own business
▶ Mind your own business!

angewurzelt • wie angewurzelt stehen
to be rooted to the spot
▶ Fear rooted me to the spot – neither the tiger nor I moved an inch.

Angst und Bange • Da kann einem ja Angst und Bange werden.
to be scared stiff (coll), to be scared to death (coll), to be frightened out of one's mind (coll), to be scared to bits (coll), to be scared shitless (vulg)
▶ When the police came and started asking me questions I was really scared stiff.

Angsthase
scaredy-cat (coll)
▶ That child is a real scaredy-cat – she is too frightened to jump into the pool.

Apfel • in den sauren Apfel beißen (müssen)
to have to bite the bullet (coll)
▶ If my company transfers me to the new factory, we'll have to bite the bullet and move away from our old home.

Apfel • für n'Appel und n'Ei
for a song
▶ They bought the house for a song.

Arm • jmd auf den Arm nehmen
to pull sbd's leg (coll), to fool sbd, to kid sbd (coll), to have sbd on (coll), to take sbd for a ride (coll), to lead sbd up the garden path (coll), to wind sbd up (coll)
▶ They really took him for a ride, making him think Sarah was in love with him when in fact she can't stand him.

Ärmel • etwas aus dem Ärmel schütteln
to do sth off the cuff (coll); to do sth just like that (coll)
▶ He never studies and in the exam he was able to answer even the most difficult questions off the cuff.

Arsch • sich in den Arsch beißen
to kick oneself (coll)
▶ I could have kicked myself when I realized we were just doing the same work twice.

Track 4

auf • das Auf und Ab
the ups and downs (coll)
▶ A big problem for her is getting used to the ups and downs of life. She seems to think that everything normally runs smoothly.

auftragen • dick auftragen
to lay it on thick (coll), to go over the top (coll), OTT (coll) (oh tee tee)
▶ Simon was telling us about how well his children played in the football match – laying it on thick, as usual.
▶ Wearing an evening gown to do the dishes is really OTT.

Auge • mit einem blauen Auge davonkommen
to get off lightly (coll)
▶ The judge gave him only six months, so he got off lightly.

Auge • ein Auge zudrücken
to turn a blind eye to sth
▶ Some schools turn a blind eye to pupils' cheating in exams, others take it very seriously.

Auge • kein Auge zutun
not to get a wink of sleep (coll)
▶ I was so worried about the news from home that I didn't get a wink of sleep all night.

Augen • unter vier Augen
in confidence
▶ We spoke to each other in confidence about the problem.

ausbaden • etwas ausbaden müssen
to face the music (coll), to take the rap (coll) (A.E.), to take the consequences
▶ He was caught committing burglary, and now he has to face the music.

außer • (vor Wut, vor Entsetzen) außer sich sein
to be beside oneself (with rage, with fear)
▶ I was beside myself with rage when I heard of the mess that had been made of my project.

aussteigen • aussteigen / ein Aussteiger sein
to drop out (coll), to be a dropout (coll)
▶ It is nothing new for young people to wish to drop out, nor for them in due course to regret having done so.

auswendig • Das kenne ich in- und auswendig.

I know it backwards (and forwards), with one hand tied behind my back

▶ Bake a cherry pie? I can do that with one hand tied behind my back. I know pies backwards and forwards.

Axt • sich wie die Axt im Walde benehmen

to be a bull in a china shop

▶ It was a delicate job, and he went at it like a bull in a china shop. The results were catastrophic.

Bahn • aus der Bahn geworfen werden

to be thrown off balance

Track 5

▶ The bad news from home threw him completely off balance.

Bahnhof • Ich versteh nur Bahnhof.

It's all Greek to me.

Balken • den Balken im eigenen Auge nicht sehen

to be a case of the pot calling the kettle black (coll),

to be a hypocrite

▶ When this government criticizes the opposition for making over-generous promises it really is a case of the pot calling the kettle black.

Bank • durch die Bank

all, without exception, the whole lot of them (coll)

▶ If we offer the children a choice between Russian and music they will all take Russian.

Bärenhunger • einen Bärenhunger haben

to be able to eat a horse (could), to be ravenous (coll),

to be starving (coll), to be famished

▶ After playing football, I am so hungry I could eat a horse.

bauen • auf jemand bauen können

to be able to count on sbd

▶ If she said she'll do it, then she'll do it – you can count on her.

Beigeschmack • einen (bitteren) Beigeschmack haben

to be tinged with, to have a touch of

▶ His memories of the army are tinged with bitterness because he was never promoted beyond major, despite an excellent record.

13

Bein • sich kein Bein ausreißen
not to work oneself to death (coll), not to break one's neck (coll), not to overdo it (coll)
▶ It's taken him six days to draft a three page document – he doesn't believe in breaking his neck to get things done, does he?

Bein • mit dem falschen / verkehrten Bein aufgestanden sein
to have got out of bed on the wrong side (coll)
▶ Sarah must have got out of bed on the wrong side this morning because she was short-tempered with her secretary.

Beine • immer wieder auf die Beine fallen
always to fall on one's feet
▶ He has been sacked from several jobs but he always manages to fall on his feet and find a better one.

Beine • sich die Beine in den Bauch stehen
(to stand) until one is ready to drop
▶ We waited outside Buckingham Palace until we were ready to drop, and never saw the Queen.

Track 6

beißen • die Farben beißen sich
to clash
▶ The wallpaper and the carpet in this restaurant clash horribly.

Berg • über den Berg sein
to be out of the woods (coll)
▶ The firm has managed to cut its losses considerably in the last quarter, but it is not out of the woods yet.

bergab • mit jmd / etwas geht es bergab

to be going downhill, to be going to the dogs (coll), to be going down the drain (coll), to be going down the tubes (coll), to be going down the pan (coll), to go to pot (coll)
▶ The school has been going down the drain ever since they made that ass Smythe the headmaster.
▶ Since his wife left him, he has gone to pot.

betucht • gut betucht sein

to be well-off (coll), to be comfortable, not to be short of a bob or two (coll)
▶ They complain endlessly of not being paid enough but most of them are very well-off.

Bierkutscher • fluchen wie ein Bierkutscher

to swear like a trooper (coll)
▶ Whenever you ask the caretaker for help he swears like a trooper and tells you that he has no time.

Bildfläche • von der Bildfläche verschwinden

to vanish into thin air
▶ We spent hours looking for the suspicious girl, but she had vanished into thin air.

Bindfäden • Es regnet Bindfäden.

it's raining cats and dogs, it's chucking it down (coll), it's pissing down (vulg)
▶ I don't want to go out, it's raining cats and dogs.

Binsen • in die Binsen gehen

to go down the drain (coll); to go phut (coll), to fall through (coll), to come to nothing
▶ The bank refused to lend us the money so the whole project went down the drain.

Blatt • Das Blatt hat sich gewendet.
The tide has turned.
▶ It is hard to date the beginning of an economic recovery. But after the event sooner or later everyone can see that the tide has turned, even if they can't say when it happened.

Blatt • kein Blatt vor den Mund nehmen
not to mince one's words, to pull one's punches (coll)
▶ My colleague doesn't mince her words. She always tells people exactly what she thinks of them.

Track 7

Blitzesschnelle • in Blitzesschnelle
like lightning, like wildfire (Verbreitung einer Nachricht usw.)
▶ The news spread like wildfire that the enemy had invaded.

Blut • Nur ruhig Blut!
Don't panic! (coll) / Stay cool! (coll) / Don't get your knickers in a twist! (vulg)

Blut • Blut und Wasser schwitzen
to be in a cold sweat
▶ At the thought of the ghost he broke into a cold sweat.

Bogen • einen großen Bogen um jmd machen
to give sbd a wide berth, to steer clear of sbd (coll)
▶ I'm steering clear of Simon at the moment, because I still owe him a hundred pounds and I can't pay him till next month.

Bombe • eine Bombe platzen lassen
to put the fat in the fire (coll), to make the shit hit the fan (vulg), to pour oil on troubled waters
▶ When the Annual Report comes out it'll really make the shit hit the fan.

Braten • den Braten riechen

to smell a rat (coll), to sense something fishy (coll)
▶ As soon as I realized how generous their offer was I smelt a rat and decided the whole thing must be a trick.

Brocken • ein harter Brocken sein

to be a tough nut to crack (coll)
▶ This is a tough nut to crack, but I know a specialist who could probably solve the problem.

Busch • auf den Busch klopfen

to sound things out (coll)
▶ I did not know how they would receive my suggestion and so I sounded the committee members out individually before I made my formal proposal.
MIND FF: to beat about the bush: um etwas herumreden

Track 8

Canossa • den Gang nach Canossa machen

to do penance
▶ When the mistake was pointed out I realized I was going to have to do penance and spend half an hour apologizing.

Chorknabe • kein Chorknabe sein

to be no angel (coll)
▶ He looks like a charming young man, but as the girls know, he is no angel.

Creme • die Creme der Gesellschaft

the creme de la creme (franz)
▶ Not all the early party members were the creme de la creme.

Track 9

Dachschaden • einen Dachschaden haben

to be not all there (coll), to have a screw loose (coll), to be bonkers (coll), to be crackers (coll), to be off one's head (coll), to be as nutty as a fruitcake, to be round the bend (coll), to be off one's rocker (coll)

▶ I listened to his idea, but I couldn't understand it at all. I don't think he's all there.

▶ Don't let Aunt Martha's complaining bother you, she's as nutty as a fruitcake.

dahinterstecken • Wer / Was steckt da dahinter?

What's the catch? / What's behind this? / Who's behind this?

▶ They're offering a free lunch? What's the catch?

Daumen • über den Daumen peilen

to hazard a rough guess at (coll), to make a rough estimate of (coll), to give a ball-park figure (A.E.) (coll) (nur Anzahl)

▶ I can hazard a rough guess at what it might cost.

Decke • an die Decke gehen

to go through the roof (coll), to blow one's top (coll), to do a wobbly (coll), to fly off the handle (coll)

▶ When he found out how badly his son had behaved at school he went through the roof.

Decke • unter einer Decke stecken

to be hand in glove with sbd (coll), to be in cahoots with sbd (coll), to be in league with sbd

▶ It was only later on that we realized that the two of them had been in cahoots with each other from the very beginning.

Dickkopf • einen Dickkopf haben

to be pigheaded (coll), pigheadedness (coll)
▶ He prolonged the negotiations for four hours through sheer pigheadedness.

Dinge • nicht mit rechten Dingen zugehen

to work sth (for sbd) (coll), to pull strings (coll), to fiddle sth (for sbd) (coll)
▶ His uncle pulled some strings and got that promotion for him.

Dingsbums

what's his / her / its name (coll), thingummygig (coll), what-do-you-call-it (whatchamacallit) (coll)
▶ You know, the woman in the candy store, what's her name?
▶ I'm up to my elbows in dishwater, bring me that ... oh ... whatchamacallit.

Track 10

Draht • auf Draht sein

to be mustard (coll)
wachsam: to be on one's toes (coll), to be on the ball (coll)
▶ We shall have to be really on our toes at this meeting – the other side have got plenty of clever ideas and we mustn't let them trick us.

wissensmäßig: to know one's stuff / onions (coll),
to be well up in sth (coll)
▶ I need a lawyer who really knows his stuff in the field of professional negligence.

Dreck • Dreck am Stecken haben
to have blotted one's copy-book (coll)
▶ He is almost the only man in politics who didn't blot his copy-book in the corrruption scandals last year.

dreizehn • Jetzt schlägt's dreizehn!
That's the last straw! / Now you've done it! / That cooks my goose!
▶ You've been late every day this week and now you tell me you're not coming to work tomorrow. That's the last straw! You're fired!

Drückeberger
faul: skiver (coll), slacker (dated)
▶ This whole department is full of skivers. Nobody ever does anything.
feig: chicken (coll)
▶ When the demonstration threatened to become a riot, he wanted to go home, and his pals accused him of being a chicken.
jemand, der leicht aufgibt: quitter (A.E.) (coll)

drum • mit allem Drum und Dran
with all the trimmings (coll), from soup to nuts (coll),
the full monty
▶ He was invited to a formal dinner party with all the trimmings.

dumm • sich nicht für dumm verkaufen lassen
not to let oneself be taken for a ride (coll)
▶ I'm certainly not going to buy one of those things! I'm not going to let myself be taken for a ride like that.

Dunst • keinen blassen Dunst haben

not to have the faintest (idea) (coll), not to have the foggiest (idea) (coll), not to have a clue (coll), not to know the first thing about it (coll)

▶ I haven't got a clue how they propose to put this project through.

durchfüttern • sich von jdm durchfüttern lassen

to freeload (coll), to sponge off (coll)

▶ He doesn't have any money, but his brother's quite successful so he freeloads off him all the time.

Dusche • wie eine kalte Dusche

to be like a slap in the face

▶ The news hit him like a slap in the face, and he lost his enthusiasm almost immediately.

Ei • jmd wie ein rohes Ei behandeln
to handle sbd with kid gloves (coll)

Track 11

▶ Throughout the debate the opposition handled us with kid gloves, as if afraid of pressing us too hard.

Ei • sich gleichen wie ein Ei dem anderen
to be as like as two peas (in a pod) (coll), to be the spitting image of each other (coll)

▶ He and his brother are as like as two peas, even though they are not twins.

Eimer • im Eimer sein
dahin: to go / to be down the drain (coll)

▶ The computer deleted the whole thing and all our work went down the drain.

kaputt: to be kaput (coll), to be bust (coll), to have had it (coll), to be a write-off (coll)

▶ I think this television has about had it – it's fifteen years old. Let's write it off and buy a flatscreen.

Plan: to be a washout (coll), to be a frost (coll)

▶ His proposal would have cost an extra five thousand pounds which we didn't have, so that plan was a washout.

Elefant • sich wie ein Elefant im Porzellanladen benehmen
to behave like a bull in a china shop (coll)

▶ Although the whole situation was very awkward, he did not stop to find out any of the details or background and went at the job like a bull in a china shop, upsetting everybody.

▶ Show some tact. Don't behave like a bull in a china shop. You don't want to upset your boss and lose the promotion.

erstunken • erstunken und erlogen

a pack of lies (coll), (a load of) bullshit (vulg),
(a load of) balls (vulg)

▶ The whole story about the prize is a load of bullshit. I don't believe it
for a moment.

Eselsohr • das Buch hat Eselsohren

to have / to get dog-ears, to be dog-eared

▶ The children love that book so much that it's getting dog-ears.

▶ He leafed through a dog-eared volume.

Eulen • Eulen nach Athen tragen

to carry (to take, to bring, to send) coals to Newcastle

▶ It's like sending coals to Newcastle to appoint another computer expert
to that office.

Track 12

fackeln • nicht lange fackeln

not to dilly-dally (coll), not to let the grass grow under one's feet
▶ Our boss doesn't dilly-dally when people repeatedly turn up late at the office. He sacks them after the second or third time.

Faden • keinen trockenen Faden am Leib haben

to look like a drowned rat, to be / to get soaked to the skin
▶ We forgot to take an umbrella and got soaked to the skin. When we finally got there we looked like drowned rats.

Fäden • die Fäden ziehen (im Hintergrund)

to pull the strings
▶ Everyone thought the son was now in charge, but his father was still pulling the strings.

fallen • jmd fallen lassen

to drop sbd like a hot potato (coll)
▶ When I find somebody's deceived me in an important matter I drop them like a hot potato.

Faust • mit der Faust auf den Tisch hauen

to put one's foot down (coll), to lay down the law
▶ It is high time you put your foot down and stopped the students cheating in exams. Soon no one will take the results seriously any more.

Faust • wie die Faust aufs Auge passen

to be bang on (coll)
▶ His argument was bang on.

Fell • jmd juckt das Fell

to be asking for it (coll), to be asking for trouble (coll)

▶ In sending police onto the streets in such numbers so soon after the riots the Home Secretary was simply asking for trouble.

Fell • jmd das Fell über die Ohren ziehen

to rip sbd off (coll)

▶ He was badly ripped off by someone who sold him a forgery.

Fett • Da hast du dein Fett weg!

That serves you right! / That'll teach you!

Fetzen • dass die Fetzen fliegen

to make the sparks fly (coll)

▶ The two sisters quarrelled with each other and really made the sparks fly.

Finger • lange Finger machen

to have sticky fingers (coll), to nick things (coll)

▶ Don't leave anything valuable on your desk – the people in this office have sticky fingers.

Fisch • stumm wie ein Fisch

to be as quiet as a mouse

Track 13
▶ He sat there all the time as quiet as a mouse.

Fische • kleine Fische

peanuts (coll)

▶ A million pounds is peanuts to a major international bank.

fix • fix und fertig sein

to be knackered (coll), to be all in (coll), to be done in (coll), to be worn out, to be bushed (coll)

▶ I came home absolutely knackered after my day's work.

Fleisch • sich ins eigene Fleisch schneiden

to cut off one's nose to spite one's face
▶ If you don't go to the party you'll be cutting off your nose to spite your face. Everyone will be there.

Flunder • platt wie eine Flunder sein

to be as flat as a pancake (coll)
▶ I sat on the hat and squashed it so that it was as flat as a pancake.

Friedenspfeife • mit jmd die Friedenspfeife rauchen

to call it pax (coll), to bury the hatchet
▶ Bob and Ray quarrelled for days; but as soon as they discovered that they had a common enemy, they decided to bury the hatchet.

Frosch • Sei kein Frosch!
Don't be such a wimp!

Fuchs • wo sich Fuchs und Hase gute Nacht sagen
right out in the sticks (coll)
▶ He comes from the sticks and doesn't know London at all.

Füße • etwas mit Füßen treten
to tear sth to pieces
▶ I don't want to tear your work to pieces, but I don't think you have done your best.

Füße • sich die Füße vertreten
to stretch one's legs (coll)
▶ After sitting in the library for four hours I went out to stretch my legs.

futsch • Futsch ist futsch und hin ist hin.
What's done is done.
It's no use crying over spilt milk. (prov)

Galgenfrist

period of grace (oft mit Fristangabe + Genitiv + grace)
▶ The landlord will give him one week's grace to pay the rent.

Gänsemarsch

to walk in single file, to walk in Indian file (coll)
▶ It's so narrow that you have to walk in single file.

geharnischt • eine geharnischte Rede halten / ein geharnischter Brief

to haul sbd over the coals (coll), a stiff letter, a stinker (coll)
▶ I hauled my neighbour over the coals because of his son's noisy parties.
▶ I wrote him a stinker the other day, but he still hasn't sent us the money he owes us.

Gehege • jmd ins Gehege kommen

to cross sbd, to get in sbd's way (coll), to cross swords with sbd
die Rechte von jmd verletzen: to encroach on sbd's preserves, to be on sbd's patch (coll)
▶ Don't cross swords with the boss – he is in a very bad mood today.

Geist • seinen Geist aufgeben

to kick the bucket (coll), to snuff it (coll), to peg out (coll), to breathe one's last, to draw one's last breath, to give up the ghost (coll)
▶ He breathed his last on 15th February after a long illness.
▶ Halfway up a steep hill the engine of the old car gave up the ghost completely.

Geld • nicht für Geld und gute Worte

not for love nor money (coll)
▶ I could not persuade them to move for love nor money.

Geld • Geld wie Heu haben

to be loaded (coll), to be rolling in it (coll), to be rolling (coll), to be made of money (coll), to have money to burn (coll)
▶ His family are absolutely rolling, you should see some of the pictures they have on their walls at home.

Gesicht • sein wahres Gesicht zeigen

to show one's true colours, to reveal one's true nature
▶ This affair has made him reveal his true colours.

Gespann • ein gutes Gespann sein

to make a good team (coll)
▶ Those two make a good team. They work very well together.

Glocke • etwas an die große Glocke hängen

to shout / trumpet sth from the housetops (coll), to broadcast, to trumpet abroad
▶ The Party press trumpeted every success from the housetops.

Track 15

Glück • auf gut Glück

on the off chance (coll)
▶ We called round on the off chance that he might be at home.

Glück • dem Glück ein wenig nachhelfen

to load the dice
▶ We can load the dice in favour of the applicant we want by requiring qualifications which she has, and which very few other people have.

Glück • Glück im Unglück haben

to be a blessing in disguise
▶ It was a blessing in disguise that we missed our plane, because a civil war broke out in the country we were heading for on the very next day.

Gott • über Gott und die Welt reden

to talk about life / about life, the universe and everything (coll) / about everything under the sun
▶ We sat for hours on the beach talking about everything under the sun.

Grab • sein eigenes Grab schaufeln

to dig one's own grave (coll)
▶ The defendant lied so unskilfully in the witness box that he dug his own grave.

Gretchenfrage • die Gretchenfrage stellen

to ask the 64,000 dollar question (coll) (A.E.)
▶ After we had discussed the details of the project, I decided to risk the 64,000 dollar question and asked him if he would be prepared to work with us permanently.

Gurgel • jmd an die Gurgel gehen

to fly at sbd's throat, to be at sbd's throat
▶ After the defeat, all the leaders were at each other's throats, blaming each other.

Gut • Unrecht Gut gedeihet nicht.

Crime doesn't pay.

gut • Es hat alles sein Gutes.

Every cloud has a silver lining. / There's some good in everything.

Haar • um ein Haar

within a hair's breadth of (coll), by the skin of one's teeth (coll), to come within an ace of (coll), to be a near (run) thing (coll), to be a close (run) thing (Schlacht, Wettkampf) (coll); to be a close shave (coll)
▶ We got through the flood by the skin of our teeth.
▶ The German armies came within a hair's breadth of capturing Moscow.
▶ The Battle of Waterloo was a near thing.
▶ I had a close shave this evening – I was almost hit by a car.

Haar • ein Haar in der Suppe finden

to find a fly in the ointment
▶ However good things seem you can rely on her to find a fly in the ointment. She is never satisfied.

Haare • etwas ist an den Haaren herbeigezogen

to be far-fetched (coll)
▶ The whole story is so far-fetched that I don't believe a word of it.

Haare • jmd die Haare vom Kopf fressen

to eat sbd out of house and home (coll)
▶ If you go on tucking in like that, you will eat us out of house and home.

Haare • sich keine grauen Haare wachsen lassen

to lose no sleep over / about sth (coll), not to worry one's head about sth (coll), not to do one's nut (in) about sth (coll)
▶ There's no point in losing any sleep over it; it'll be all right in time.

Haare • jmd stehen die Haare zu Berge

sbd's hair stands on end
▶ The tale he told was enough to make your hair stand on end.
Adjektiv: hair-raising
▶ It's a hair-raising story.

Hals • jmd / etwas am Hals haben

to be lumbered with sbd / sth (coll), to be saddled with sbd / sth (coll), to have sbd / sth on one's hands
▶ My daughter said she wanted a dog, but I'm lumbered with him – she never takes him for walks.

Hals • zum Hals heraushängen

to be sick and tired of (coll), to be sick to death of (coll), to be cheesed off with (coll), to be pissed off with (vulg)
▶ I'm pissed off with cricket – I'm going to take up tennis instead.

Hand • etwas unter der Hand bekommen

to get sth on the black market, to get sth under the counter (coll), through channels (coll)
▶ We got the food on the black market. We paid for it with American cigarettes.

Track 17

Hand • etwas aus erster Hand haben

to have sth first hand (coll), to have sth straight from source (coll), to have sth straight from the horse's mouth (coll), to have sth hot off the press (coll)
▶ Caroline is getting married! I heard it first hand, from her own lips.

Hand • seine Hand im Spiel haben

to have a finger in the pie (negativ) (coll), to have a say in the business (coll)
▶ That fellow always wants to know what's going on. He likes to have a finger in every pie.

Hand • für jmd / etwas die Hand ins Feuer legen

to stake one's life on sth
▶ She won't let you down. I'd stake my life on that.

Hände • zwei linke Hände haben
to be all thumbs (coll)
▶ You clumsy ass, you're all thumbs today. Can't you even tighten a screw?

Hände • in die Hände spucken
to get / knuckle down to sth (coll)
▶ I know you don't like to clean your room; but if you knuckle down, you'll have it done in next to no time.

händeringend • händeringend nach etwas / jmd suchen
to search for sbd / sth high and low (coll)
▶ Where have you been? I've been searching for you high and low.

Handtuch • das Handtuch werfen
to throw in the towel (coll)
▶ Sometimes I feel like throwing in the towel. I do all this for these people, and I never get one word of thanks.

Handumdrehen • im Handumdrehen
in less than no time (coll), in next to no time (coll), in a jiffy (coll), in two ticks (coll), in a trice, in a (split) second (coll), in a twinkling (coll)
▶ With his help we got the work done in a jiffy.

Hansdampf • Hansdampf in allen Gassen sein
to be a jack-of-all-trades (coll)
▶ He calls himself an electrician, but he is really a jack-of-all-trades.
He can do most repairs.

Harnisch • in Harnisch geraten
to fly into a rage
▶ When he heard about the debt his son was in he flew into a rage and
threw him out of the house.

hart • wenn es hart auf hart kommt
**if push comes to shove (coll), if it comes down to it (coll),
when it comes to the crunch (coll)**
▶ He'll help us if push comes to shove and we're really desperate.

Hase • ein alter Hase sein
to be an old campaigner (coll), to be an old hand (coll)

Track 18

▶ None of us had tackled such a job before so we listened closely to what
the old campaigner had to say.

Hasenfuß • ein Hasenfuß sein
to be yellow (coll), to be chicken (coll)
▶ He refused to fight and all the people in town called him yellow.

Haubitze • voll wie eine Haubitze sein
to be drunk as a lord (coll)
▶ It's no use calling for the caretaker. He's drunk as a lord again.

Haus • ein fideles Haus sein
to be a laugh (coll), to be a bundle of laughs (coll)
▶ His brother is a laugh – he never takes anything seriously.

haushoch • jmd haushoch überlegen sein

to stand head and shoulders above sbd (in / at sth), to be miles / streets ahead of sbd (coll) (in / at sth), to knock sbd into a cocked hat (coll) (at sth), to be able to … the socks off sbd (coll), to be sbd to whom you cannot hold a candle (coll)

▶ As an actress she can't hold a candle to her mother.

▶ The visiting team can play the socks off the home side.

Haut • sich seiner Haut wehren

to stand up for oneself (coll), to stand one's ground, not to give / budge an inch (coll)

▶ When they wanted to reduce her salary, she didn't give an inch and simply refused to agree.

Hebel • alle Hebel in Bewegung setzen

to leave no stone unturned

▶ He left no stone unturned in his efforts to obtain a transfer to the London office.

heiß • ganz heiß auf etwas sein

to be very keen on sth

▶ They were really very keen to see the film; but once they saw it, they were disappointed.

Heller • keinen roten Heller besitzen

not to have a penny to one's name, not to have a bean (coll), not to have a brass farthing (coll)

▶ They do not have a penny to their names and cannot possibly afford to do what you are suggesting.

Hemd • Das letzte Hemd hat keine Taschen.

You can't take it with you.

▶ I'm treating myself to a trip around the world. Sure, it's expensive, but you can't take it with you.

hereinfallen • auf jmd hereinfallen
to fall for sbd / sth hook, line and sinker (coll)
▶ I fell for him hook, line and sinker.

Herz • das Herz auf der Zunge haben
to wear one's heart on one's sleeve (Shakespeare: Othello)
▶ He wears his heart on his sleeve, so we all knew he was very upset.

Herz • jmd / etwas auf Herz und Nieren prüfen
to put sbd / sth through his / her / its paces
▶ We put the new computer programme through its paces.

Herzen • aus seinem Herzen keine Mördergrube machen
not to mince one's words
▶ I did not mince my words, and I told her exactly what I thought of her dirty tricks.

Heulen • mit Heulen und Zähneklappern
with fear and trembling (bibl)
▶ He confessed with fear and trembling that he was the father of the child.

Track 19

hieb • hieb- und stichfest sein
rock solid
▶ His alibi is rock solid, and cannot be shaken.

Himmel • jmd den Himmel auf Erden versprechen
to promise sbd the moon (coll), to promise sbd heaven on earth
▶ As soon as the campaign begins the politicians will start promising everybody the moon.

hinten • jmd hintenan stellen
to be an also-ran (coll)
▶ Her boss considered her an also-ran and never put her up for promotion.

hinten • es jmd hinten und vorne reinstecken

to spoon-feed (coll)
▶ If you continue to spoon-feed the boy, he'll never stand on his own two feet.

Hinterhand • etwas in der Hinterhand haben

to have sth up one's sleeve (coll)
▶ He's very clever and I don't trust him. You never know what he's got up his sleeve.

Hintertürchen • sich ein Hintertürchen offen halten

to leave oneself a loop-hole (coll), to leave oneself a way out (coll), to leave oneself a line of retreat, to find / exploit a loop-hole
▶ He more or less committed himself but left himself a loop-hole, saying he would have to talk to his boss about it first.

Hinz • Hinz und Kunz

every Tom, Dick and Harry (coll), all and sundry (coll)
▶ I don't want to have this project spoilt by letting every Tom, Dick and Harry stick his nose in.

hochleben • jmd hochleben lassen

to give sbd three cheers
▶ We gave the footballers three cheers after they came in from the field.

Hochzeiten • auf zwei Hochzeiten tanzen

to be in two places at once / at one time
▶ They want me to work in the accounts department and in the registry, but I can't be in two places at once.
▶ Harry's wedding or Sandra's debut – I sure wish I were twins and could be in two places at once.

Hölle • jmd die Hölle heiß machen
to give sbd hell (coll)
▶ He's giving us hell because he wants his money back from us.

Holzweg • auf dem Holzweg sein
to be on the wrong track (coll)
▶ You are on the wrong track there! My dog didn't bite the postman!

Track 20

Honig • Das ist kein Honigschlecken.
not to be a bed of roses (coll), to be no doddle (coll)
▶ Working with him is no doddle, he's a slave-driver.

Honigkuchenpferd • wie ein Honigkuchenpferd strahlen
to beam from ear to ear, to grin from ear to ear, to grin like a Cheshire cat (Lewis Carroll)
▶ After he heard he had won the prize he went off grinning from ear to ear.

Hopfen • Da ist Hopfen und Malz verloren.
He is a hopeless case.

Horn • ins gleiche Horn blasen
to take the same line / view / attitude, to sing the same tune (coll)
▶ Every party in the coalition has been singing the same tune for so long it's now difficult to tell them apart.

Hörner • sich die Hörner abstoßen
to sow one's wild oats (coll)
▶ He sowed his wild oats before his marriage, and now he is a most respectable husband.

Hühnchen • mit jmd noch ein Hühnchen zu rupfen haben

to have a bone to pick with sbd (coll)

▶ Hey, I've got a bone to pick with you! Why didn't you turn up last week? I waited for an hour and a half.

Hund • ein krummer Hund sein

to be a crook (coll), to be bent (coll)

▶ Don't trust him, he's a crook!

Hungertuch • am Hungertuch nagen

to be unable to keep the wolf from the door (coll)

▶ I have my income from my American investments and I earn a bit with my articles for the newspapers, and that is enough to keep the wolf from the door.

Hut • den Hut vor jmd ziehen

to take one's hat off to someone (coll)

▶ I take my hat off to those who died in the fight for freedom.

Track 21

Innerste • bis ins Innerste getroffen sein

to be cut to the quick
▶ His remark about my daughter cut me to the quick.

Jahre • alle Jahre wieder

year in, year out (coll)
▶ Year in, year out, Uncle George came to stay for Christmas.

Jammerlappen • ein Jammerlappen sein

**to be a cry-baby (coll) (wenn es zum Weinen kommt),
to be a wimp (coll), to be a sissy (coll)**
▶ Don't be a wimp, put on those gloves and get into the ring!

jeder • Jeder ist sich selbst der Nächste.

Look after / out for Number One. / Every man for himself!
▶ He'll never lose his job. He knows how to look out for Number One!

Jordan • über den Jordan gehen

to vanish into thin air (forever), to go West (coll)
▶ That's what happens when you tidy up – half my papers vanish into thin air and I'll never see them again.

Jubeljahr • alle Jubeljahre (einmal)

**once in a blue moon (coll), once in a month of Sundays (coll),
once every million years (coll)**
▶ I've no idea how he is – I see him only once in a blue moon.

Judaslohn • Judaslohn (bekommen)

(to get one's) thirty pieces of silver / blood money
▶ After betraying his friends, he collected his thirty pieces of silver.

41

Kacke • die Kacke ist am Dampfen
the shit is going to hit the fan (vulg)
▶ The boss has just found out about the missing money, and now the shit is going to hit the fan.

Kaffee • Das ist doch kalter Kaffee!
That is old hat. (coll)
▶ Oh, please, not that song again! That song is just old hat.

Kaffee • Dem hat man wohl was in den Kaffee getan!
He must be joking! / He must be kidding! / He must be having you / me / them (usw.) on! / He must be pulling my / your (usw.) leg.
▶ He couldn't have said that ... he must be joking! Are you sure he's not pulling your leg?

Kaiser • Wo nichts ist, hat der Kaiser sein Recht verloren. (prov)
You can't get blood out of a stone.
▶ He's bankrupt and going to prison. We'll never see our money. You can't get blood out of a stone.

Kanonen • mit Kanonen auf Spatzen schießen
to use a sledge-hammer to crack a nut (coll)
▶ In calling out the army to deal with the rioting schoolchildren the authorities were using a sledge-hammer to crack a nut.

Kanonenrohr • Heiliges Kanonenrohr!
Good grief!

Karren • den Karren aus dem Dreck ziehen
to clean up the mess (coll), to put things straight (coll), to get things back on the rails (coll)
▶ After my holiday it took me a couple of weeks to clean up the mess. My deputy had made every possible mistake while I had been away.

Karte • alles auf eine Karte setzen
to put all one's eggs in one basket (coll), to stake everything on one card (coll)
▶ We have to succeed today because we have put all our eggs in one basket.
▶ Diversify, diversify … don't put all your eggs in one basket!

Käseblatt
rag (coll), scandal sheet (coll)
▶ That newspaper once had pretentions to being a serious journal but it's nothing but a scandal sheet now – sport and sex.

Kasse • getrennte Kasse machen
to go Dutch
▶ I can't afford to take you all out to dinner – we shall have to go Dutch.

Katze • die Katze aus dem Sack lassen
to let the cat out of the bag (coll), to spill the beans (coll), to give the game away (coll)

Track 23
▶ He gave the game away about our Christmas surprise for the children.

Katze • die Katze im Sack kaufen

to buy a pig in a poke (coll)
▶ We have to show the people what we're offering because nobody is buying a pig in a poke nowadays.

Katze • wie die Katze um den heißen Brei herumschleichen

to pussyfoot, to beat about the bush
▶ Stop pussyfooting around and say what you want.
▶ Stop beating about the bush and tell me if I've won the prize.

Katzensprung • Das ist ein Katzensprung von hier.

That is a stone's throw from here.
▶ We'll get there in no time, it's just a stone's throw away.

Kieker • jmd auf dem Kieker haben

to be in sbd's bad books (coll), to have got one's eye on sbd
▶ He's got his eye on me. I daren't go near him.
▶ I am really in his bad books and I have to watch my step.

Kind • das Kind beim Namen nennen

to call a spade a spade (coll), to be perfectly frank
▶ To call a spade a spade, what you are doing is dishonest.

Kind • mit Kind und Kegel

everything but the kitchen sink (coll), me and mine / you and yours / he and his / she and hers / they and theirs
▶ We set off on holiday with everything but the kitchen sink.
▶ I am giving you notice to quit: you and yours must be out of this flat by the end of next month.

Kinderschuhe • noch in den Kinderschuhen stecken

to be still in the early stages/days, to be in embryo, to be still in diapers (A.E.) (coll)

▶ This new project is still in the early stages and I don't think we can expect a return on our investment for some time yet.

▶ It is still early days, so we can't expect to earn anything with this project just yet.

Kippe • etwas steht auf der Kippe

to be hanging by a thread (coll), to be in the balance, to be on a knife edge (coll)

▶ The patient's survival has been hanging by a thread since the last operation.

Kirche • die Kirche im Dorf lassen

to draw the line (coll)

▶ We can let the children drink and smoke if they must, but I'm not having them take drugs – you have to draw the line somewhere.

Klappe • eine große Klappe haben

to be cheeky (coll), to be mouthy (coll), to get fresh (A.E.) (coll)

Track 24

▶ That child is horribly cheeky to her teachers.

Klapperstorch • an den Klapperstorch glauben

to believe in fairies (coll)

▶ He is twelve and he still believes in fairies!

Klatsch • Klatsch und Tratsch

tittle tattle (coll), chitchat (coll), gossip (coll), tit-bits (coll), scuttlebutt (A.E.) (coll)

▶ The women's magazines are full of chitchat about the Royal Family.

Klemme • in der Klemme sein / sitzen
to be in a spot (coll), to be in a fix (coll), to be in a tight corner (coll), to be in a jam (coll), to be in a fine mess, to be up a gum-tree (coll), to be in the shit (vulg), to be in deep shit (vulg), to be up shit creek (without a paddle) (vulg)
▶ If we can't get help, we shall be up shit creek without a paddle.

Klette • sich wie eine Klette an jmd hängen / eine Klette sein
to stick to sbd like glue / a limpet (coll)
▶ My daughter's new boyfriend sticks to her like a limpet and doesn't give her any time on her own at all.

Klotz • jmd ein Klotz am Bein sein
to be a millstone round sbd's neck
▶ The present organisation is a millstone round our neck. We shall have to get rid of it and start from scratch if we want to get anything done.

Knie • seine Knie waren wie Wachs
his knees turned to jelly (coll)
▶ When he heard that the headmaster wanted to speak to him his knees turned to jelly.

Kniff • den Kniff bei etwas heraushaben
to have got the hang / knack of sth (coll)
▶ I'll just see how you get on with this machine until I know you've got the hang of it.
▶ This machine isn't hard to handle, but I'll stand by until I know you've got the hang of it.

Kopf • nicht auf den Kopf gefallen sein
to be no fool (coll), not to have been born yesterday (coll), to have no flies on one (coll)
▶ You can't trick me, I'm no fool. I wasn't born yesterday.

Kopf • nicht wissen, wo einem der Kopf steht

**not to know if one is coming or going (coll) / whether one is
on one's head or one's heels (coll)**
▶ My friends came and went so often over Christmas that I didn't know
if I was coming or going.

Kopf • jmd vor den Kopf stoßen

to turn sbd down flat (coll)
▶ I asked that girl for a dance, but she turned me down flat.

Kopf • jmd den Kopf waschen

**to give somebody a lecture, to give sbd a rocket (coll), to have
sbd up on one's carpet (coll), to carpet sbd (coll), to give sbd
an earful (coll), to give sbd a dressing-down (coll), to bawl
sbd out (coll) (A.E.), to give sbd a bollocking (vulg), to take /
call sbd out on the carpet**
▶ It's the third time this week that John has been late. Our teacher gave
him a proper dressing-down. John really got an earful!

Kopf • sich den Kopf zerbrechen

to rack one's brains (coll)
▶ We racked our brains to find a solution to the problem, but without
success.

Korn • jmd aufs Korn nehmen

to put to the test
▶ The Opposition have decided to put the Prime Minister's reputation
for social awareness to the test.

Track 25

kotzen • Das ist zum Kotzen!
That is shitty! / Disgusting! / It makes you sick!

Kragenweite • Der / Das ist nicht meine Kragenweite!

That's not my cup of tea. (coll) / That's not my idea of fun. (coll) /
That's not my bag. (coll)

▶ Hiking in the rain is not my cup of tea.

kratzen • Das kratzt mich nicht!

It's no skin off my nose!

Kreise • etwas zieht Kreise

to make waves

▶ The scandal about her adulterous affair made waves in the whole village.

kugeln • sich kugeln / kringeln vor Lachen

to laugh till one cries (coll), to laugh oneself to death (coll),
to laugh oneself silly (coll), to split one's sides laughing (coll)

▶ They laughed themselves to death over the news.

Track 26

Laden • den Laden schmeißen
to run the whole show (coll)
▶ That girl runs the whole show on her own – and she has only been with us three weeks.

Ladenhüter • ein Ladenhüter sein
to be a flop, sth won't sell
▶ This range of goods is a complete flop: nobody is buying them.
▶ We can't shift this new tin opener. It won't sell.

Land • kein Land sehen
to see no light at the end of the tunnel (coll)
▶ As an economy measure the light at the end of the tunnel has been turned off until further notice. (Londoner Witz während der wirtschaftlichen Talfahrt 1992)

Länder • Andere Länder, andere Sitten. (prov)
When in Rome, do as the Romans do. (prov)

Lappen • durch die Lappen gehen
to slip through one's fingers (from one's grasp)
▶ We let the opportunity slip through our fingers and it will never come again.

Leben • etwas für sein Leben gern tun
to be mad on sth (coll), to be mad keen on sth (coll), to be crazy about sth (coll)
▶ She is crazy about Heine, and reads nothing else at the moment.

Leben • das nackte Leben retten

to escape in what one stands up in (coll), to escape in nothing but the clothes on your back (coll)
▶ He had escaped from prison in nothing but the clothes on his back, and one of his first requirements was a pair of trousers and a shirt.

Leckermaul • ein Leckermaul sein

to have a sweet tooth
▶ Give her a box of chocolates. She has a sweet tooth and will really enjoy your gift.

Leder • jmd ans Leder wollen

to nail sbd for sth (coll)
▶ The police were very eager to nail him for the burglary, but he was able to prove he had been elsewhere at the time.

Leder • vom Leder ziehen

to pull out all the stops (coll)
▶ The Leader of the Opposition pulled out all the stops, but his speech still failed to convince the MPs.

Lehrgeld • Lehrgeld zahlen müssen

to have to learn the hard way (coll)
▶ Nobody ever gave me any tips on how to do this – I had to learn the hard way.

Leiche • eine Leiche im Keller haben

to have a skeleton in the cupboard (coll)
▶ That family has got a lot of skeletons in the cupboard they think nobody knows about.

Leichen • über Leichen gehen

to stick at nothing (coll)
▶ He'll stick at nothing to get his own way – he is quite ruthless.

Leid • Wie das Leiden Christi aussehen

to look like death warmed up / over (coll), to look shitty (vulg), to look washed out (coll)

Track 27

▶ David has flu; he came to the office looking really shitty and I sent him home again.

Leim • jmd auf den Leim gehen / kriechen

to be conned (coll), to be fooled (coll), to be had (coll)

▶ We were had! They conned us out of seven thousand pounds.

Leseratte • eine Leseratte sein

to be a bookworm (coll)

▶ He is a real bookworm. You never see him without a book in his hand.

Leuchte • keine Leuchte sein

to be no great shakes (at sth) (coll)

▶ I am no great shakes at Latin, I'm afraid.

Leute • Es ist nicht wie bei armen Leuten.

We're not quite broke yet.

Leute • geschiedene Leute

not to be on speaking terms (coll), to have fallen out (coll)

▶ Since we quarrelled during the summer, we have not been on speaking terms.

Licht • jmd geht ein Licht auf

to dawn on sbd (coll), to tumble to the fact that (coll), the scales fall from sbd's eyes (coll), the penny drops (coll)

▶ "It suddenly dawned on me that we were going to have to invest yet more money in the project." – "And when did the scales fall from your eyes?"

Licht • jmd hinters Licht führen

to pull the wool over sbd's eyes
▶ Denials by the company of having politicians on the payroll are designed to pull the wool over the eyes of the public.

Licht • sich ins rechte Licht setzen

to sing one's own praises, to blow one's own trumpet (coll), to make sure one's efforts are noticed
▶ He blew his own trumpet vociferously about his achievements in office, but nevertheless he was not re-elected.

Lied • Davon kann ich ein Lied singen!

I know a thing or two about that (coll), I could tell you a thing or two about that (coll), I could write a book about that (coll)
▶ I could tell you a thing or two about trying to deal with this firm. For instance, nobody is ever in the office after five pm.

Linie • keine klare Linie vertreten

to chop and change (coll)
▶ He changes his mind every two minutes, and you can't rely on him to keep to his opinion at all, he chops and changes the whole time.

links • etwas mit links machen

to find sth a doddle (coll)
▶ Mathematics is very simple. The last exam I did I found a doddle.

Track 28

List • mit List und Tücke

by hook or by crook, by low cunning, chicanery
▶ Some of these estate agents' methods are pure chicanery. They'll get you to sign a lease by hook or by crook.

Loch • saufen wie ein Loch
to drink like a fish (coll), to be a boozer
▶ He drinks like a fish – you can smell whisky on his breath from eleven o'clock every morning.

Loch • ein Loch aufreißen, um ein anderes zu stopfen
to rob Peter to pay Paul
▶ We urgently need more people for the Alpha project – but we mustn't take them from the Beta project, because that would be robbing Peter to pay Paul.

Loch • auf / aus dem letzten Loch pfeifen
to be on one's last legs
▶ My radio is on its last legs. I think I need a new one.

loslegen • loslegen mit etwas
to fire away (coll), to shoot (coll) (bes. Fragen stellen)
▶ You wanted to tell me about your experience in Russia so fire away.

loswerden • etwas loswerden wollen (von der Seele reden)
to want to unburden oneself, to want to get sth off one's chest (coll)
▶ She could see something was troubling her son, but he didn't seem to want to talk about it. She waited patiently until he was ready to unburden himself.

Lot • wieder ins Lot bringen
to smooth things over (coll), to patch things up (coll), to make amends
▶ I have been trying to smooth things over between those two for years, but I'm afraid they simply do not want to make amends.

Lückenbüßer • der Lückenbüßer sein
to be (sbd's) stand-in (coll), to stand in for sbd (coll)
▶ Mr Trundlehumper is on holiday and I'm standing in for him.

Luft • Die Luft ist rein!
The coast is clear!

Luft • seinen Gefühlen Luft machen
to let off steam (coll), to give vent to one's feelings
▶ He let off steam for half an hour about the fact that he had not got the promotion he wanted.

Lunge • sich die Lunge aus dem Hals schreien
to shout oneself hoarse (coll), to scream one's head off (coll)
▶ The football fans shouted themselves hoarse during the match.

Lust • ganz nach Lust und Laune
as the fancy takes you (coll), just as you like (coll)
▶ You can dine at seven or eight, as the fancy takes you.

Made • wie die Made im Speck leben
to be as happy as a pig in clover (coll), to be as snug as a bug in a rug (coll)

Track 29

▶ He is as snug as a bug in a rug in Austria – he has a good job, lots of friends – why should he want to come home to England?

Maul • sich das Maul über etwas zerreißen
to sound off about sth (coll)
▶ He sounded off about the bad bus services for about half an hour.

Mauseloch • sich ins Mauseloch verkriechen
to want the ground to swallow one up (coll), to want to crawl into a corner and hide, to be able to (could, could have) die from embarrassment
▶ When I found out that he knew, I could have died from embarrassment.

mausetot • mausetot sein
to be as dead as a doornail (coll), to be as dead as a dodo (coll)
▶ The transmitter was as dead as a doornail.

Mäuschen • Mäuschen spielen mögen
to want to be a fly on the wall (coll)
▶ I would love to be a fly on the wall in that meeting and see how the quarrel develops.

Miene • keine Miene verziehen
ohne die Gefühle zu verraten: without batting an eyelid (coll)
▶ When the managing director starts talking nonsense we have to sit there without batting an eyelid.
kaltblütig reagieren oder handeln: without turning a hair (coll)
▶ The boss was so ruthless he could sack sixty employees without turning a hair.

Miene • gute Miene zum bösen Spiel machen

to make the best of a bad job (coll), to grin and bear it (coll)
▶ We're not going to be able to do this job the way we wanted, because the head office didn't agree. Still, we shall have to grin and bear it and do the best we can.

mir • mir nichts, dir nichts

just like that (coll), as bold as brass (coll), as cool as be damned (coll)
▶ In he came, as bold as brass, and asked if he could take over my office.

Mond • jmd auf den Mond schießen wollen

to wish sbd to the devil (coll)
▶ I was so annoyed I told him to go to the devil.

Mücke • aus einer Mücke einen Elefanten machen

to make a mountain out of a mole-hill (coll)
▶ It is not so difficult as they all seem to think. They are making mountains out of mole-hills.

Mund • sich den Mund verbrennen

to burn one's fingers (coll), to get one's fingers burnt (coll), to get into hot water (coll), to come a cropper (coll)
▶ I got into hot water over my critical report and I certainly don't want to tell the truth to these people any more – I'd just get my fingers burnt again.
▶ You came a cropper over that one, didn't you.

Murmeltier • schlafen wie ein Murmeltier

to sleep like a log / top (coll), to be dead to the world (coll)
▶ Don't wake her if she's still dead to the world.

Nacht • bei Nacht und Nebel
at dead of night, in the middle of the night

► If you're out on the streets at dead of night in a small town, of course the police will take notice.

Track 30

Nacht • hässlich wie die Nacht sein
to be as ugly as sin (coll)

► Have you seen her sister? She is as ugly as sin – I can't imagine anyone dancing with her.

Nachtigall • Nachtigall ick hör dir trapsen!
Aha, I know what's cooking! (coll)

Nagel • den Nagel auf den Kopf treffen
eine Person mit Kritik treffen: to strike home (coll)

► When he said that she was not looking after her husband properly that struck home.

einen Punkt genau treffen: to hit the nail on the head (coll)

► When you say we simply don't have enough people prepared to work for us, you have hit the nail on the head. That is precisely the problem.

Name • Mein Name ist Hase.
Search me! / I'm damned / blowed if I know!

Nase • die Nase voll haben
to be fed up with sth / sbd
▶ I can't go there anymore. I'm so fed up with their constant complaining.

nehmen • Woher nehmen, wenn nicht stehlen?
Do you think they grow on trees?
▶ No, I can't buy you everything you see in the fashion magazines; do you think money grows on trees?

Neid • grün vor Neid sein
to be green with envy (coll)
▶ When I saw his new car I went green with envy.

Track 31

Nesseln • sich in die Nesseln setzen
to be on a sticky wicket
▶ If you tell him the truth, you could find yourself on a sticky wicket.

neugeboren • sich wie neugeboren fühlen
to feel on top of the world (coll), to feel on cloud nine (coll),
to feel like a new man / woman / person
▶ After arriving in Paris for my holiday, I felt on top of the world.

nichts • nach nichts aussehen
to look very ordinary, to not look anything special
▶ The car doesn't look anything special, but it is more powerful than it appears.

nichts • vor dem Nichts stehen
to stand on the edge of the abyss, to be faced with ruin,
to have ruin stare one in the face, to teeter on the brink (coll)
▶ This business is teetering on the brink of collapse.

niet • alles, was nicht niet- und nagelfest ist

everything that is not nailed down (coll)

▶ The burglars took everything that was not nailed down.

Not • wenn Not am Mann ist

if push comes to shove (coll), if the worst comes to the worst (coll)

▶ If push comes to shove, we'll have to work through the night to get this finished on time.

Not • in der Not frisst der Teufel Fliegen

Beggars cannot be choosers.

Nummer • auf Nummer Sicher gehen

just to be on the safe side ...

▶ I'll ring him and ask, just to be on the safe side.

oben • Mir steht es bis oben.

**I am sick and tired of it. (coll) / I am fed up (to the back teeth)
with it. (coll)**
▶ I'm sick and tired of listening to her complain about her job.

Ohr • ganz Ohr sein

to be all ears (coll)
▶ Go ahead and tell me about it; I'm all ears.

Ohr • sich aufs Ohr legen

**to have a snooze (coll), to have a kip (coll), to snooze (coll),
to kip (coll), to crash out (coll), to have forty winks (coll), to have
(take) a nap**
▶ We drank so much beer at lunchtime we all crashed out in the afternoon.
▶ Two glasses of wine at lunch and I need an afternoon snooze.

Ohren • tauben Ohren predigen

**it's like talking to a brick wall, to talk to the wall (coll),
to preach to deaf ears**
▶ I have told you to buy a new coat over and over again but I might just
as well talk to the wall – you never take any notice.

Ohren • viel um die Ohren haben

to be up to one's eyes in work (coll), to be up to one's eyes in things (coll), to be up to one's eyes in it (coll), to have a lot on one's plate (coll)

▶ I can't possibly come round tomorrow: I'm up to my eyes in work.

Otto • Otto Normalverbraucher

the man (woman) in the street; the average consumer

▶ Most advertizing campaigns are directed at the man in the street, your average consumer.

Otto • den flotten Otto haben

to have (get) gippy tummy (coll), to have (get) Delhi belly (coll), to suffer from Montezuma's revenge (coll), to have (get) the runs (vulg), to have (get) the trots (vulg)

▶ He'd have an awful time if he went to India – he always gets the runs after eating curry.

packen • Pack dich!
Clear off! (coll) / **Beat it!** (coll) / **Sod off!** (vulg) /
Piss off! (very vulg) / **Fuck off!** (very vulg)

Palme • jmd auf die Palme bringen
to make sbd see red (coll), to make sbd's blood boil (coll)
▶ The article in today's newspaper made me really see red! I've written
a letter to the editor to protest.

Pantoffel • unterm Pantoffel stehen
to be under sbd's thumb (coll)
▶ If he marries her, he'll be under her thumb for the rest of his life.

passen • wie angegossen passen
to fit like a glove, to fit to a T
▶ That dress fits you like a glove (fits you to a T).

Pauke • auf die Pauke hauen
**sich vergnügen: to paint the town red (coll), to really go for it,
to let one's hair down, to rave it up (feiern)**
▶ It was Saturday night and the girls decided to really go for it, so
they painted the town red, got smashed and came home at three o'clock
in the morning.
angeben: to show off
▶ He was showing off all evening – talking about the famous people he's met.

Pech • wie Pech und Schwefel zusammenhalten
to be as thick as thieves
▶ They were at school together and remained as thick as thieves all their
lives.

Perle • Da wird dir keine Perle aus der Krone fallen!

It won't kill you.

▶ Try and mend your shirts yourself – it won't kill you.

Pest • jmd die Pest an den Hals wünschen

to wish sbd would drop dead (coll)

▶ I wish he'd just drop dead – he does nothing but criticize.

Pest • jmd / etwas wie die Pest hassen

to loathe sbd/sth, to hate sbd's guts (coll)

▶ She hates my guts and won't do me any favours.

Pfad • auf dem Pfad der Tugend wandeln

to keep (to stick) to the straight and narrow (path) (bibl)

Track 34

▶ She stuck (kept) to the straight and narrow (path) all her life, avoiding pubs, drugs and men.

Pfau • eitel wie ein Pfau sein

to be as proud as a peacock (coll) / as vain as a peacock (coll), to be puffed up with pride, to plume oneself, to give oneself airs

▶ She was as proud as a peacock after she won the competition.

Pferd • Das hält kein Pferd aus.
It's more than flesh and blood can stand.

Pferde • Immer langsam mit den jungen Pferden!
Easy does it! (coll) / Hold your horses! (coll)

Pferde • mit jmd Pferde stehlen können
to be a good (real) sport (coll); to be a great guy (coll),
to be a great bloke (coll)
▶ He's a great bloke, you can always rely on him to help out.
▶ He's a good sport, you can always rely on him to help out.

Pferdefuß • einen Pferdefuß haben
there is a catch in it, it's got a snag (coll)
▶ So where's the catch? There have got to be some snags; it's far too cheap otherwise.

Pfingstochse • herausgeputzt wie ein Pfingstochse
to be dressed / done / dolled up to the nines (coll) (dated),
to be dressed to kill
▶ Jane went to the disco dressed to kill and came back with a broad assortment of possible boyfriends.

Pflock • einen Pflock zurückstecken
to back-pedal a bit (coll)
▶ First of all they said they wouldn't pay anything, but then they back-pedalled a bit and offered to cover our expenses.

Phrase • leere (hohle) Phrasen dreschen
hot air (coll), empty words
▶ The Prime Minister made a speech – all hot air as usual.

Pike • etwas von der Pike auf lernen

to learn sth / to start sth from scratch (coll)
▶ He's really learnt his craft from scratch.

Pontius • von Pontius zu Pilatus laufen / geschickt werden

to go / to be sent from pillar to post (coll)
▶ I was sent from pillar to post trying to find out what form I was supposed to fill in.

Porzellan • viel Porzellan zerschlagen

to leave blood on the carpet (coll)
▶ After the argument with the boss there was a lot of blood left on the carpet – lots of people were very upset.

Primel • eingehen wie eine Primel

to wither / pine away (and die)
▶ If I had to live in that damp and dirty flat, I would just wither away (and die).

Pudel • des Pudels Kern

the heart of the matter, the long and the short of it (coll)
▶ The long and the short of it is, he took the job for the money.

pudelwohl • sich pudelwohl fühlen

to feel as fit as a fiddle (health) (coll), to feel like a million dollars (coll) (dated), to be full of beans (coll) (dated), to be on top of the world
▶ He's just come back from a skiing holiday and now he feels as fit as a fiddle.
▶ He's fallen in love again, so naturally he feels on top of the world.

Punkt • den Punkt aufs i setzen

to give sth the finishing touch
▶ To give the party a finishing touch, he booked a live band.

Quecksilber • ein Quecksilber sein / Quecksilber im Leibe haben
to have the fidgets (coll), to be a fidget (coll), to have ants in
your pants (A.E.), to be unable to sit still
▶ That boy is such a fidget! He can never sit still for two minutes together.

Track 36

Racker • ein Racker sein
to be a real handful (coll)
▶ She is only three but she is getting to be a real handful. She dug up all the rose bushes last week.

Räder • unter die Räder kommen
to go to the dogs (coll), to go off the rails (coll), to come to grief
▶ He did well at school but at university he went right off the rails: too much drink, too many girls.

Rage • jmd bringt etwas in Rage
to get hot under the collar
▶ You'd better stop smoking here. She hates it and is getting hot under the collar.

Ränke • Ränke schmieden
to hatch a plot, to work up a conspiracy
▶ She's always hatching plots to secure her divide-and-rule control of the office.

Rappel • einen Rappel haben
to be in a foul mood (coll), to be in a temper
▶ My husband has been in a foul mood ever since he got home from work. Something went wrong at the office today.

rar • sich rar machen
to be out of circulation (coll), to make oneself scarce (coll)
▶ Christine has been out of circulation for weeks, working for her exams. None of her friends have seen her.

Raubbau • (mit seiner Gesundheit) Raubbau treiben

(normalerweise gleichzeitig fleißig arbeiten und zu viel Spaß haben)

to burn the candle at both ends

▶ She works twelve hours a day and then goes clubbing. If she keeps burning the candle at both ends, she'll make herself ill.

Recht • an den Rechten geraten

to meet one's match, to meet one's Waterloo

▶ He thought he could beat any of us at tennis but he met his Waterloo when he played Paul. Paul beat him 6-2, 6-0.

Rede • langer Rede kurzer Sinn

to put it in a nutshell ..., the long and the short of it is ...,

keeping it short and sweet (coll) ...

▶ I could get down on my knees and recite a poem or do a song and dance; but to put it in a nutshell, will you marry me?

Rede • jmd Rede und Antwort stehen

to face the music

▶ Dad will hit the roof when he hears I failed the exam. I guess I better go home and face the music.

Regel • nach allen Regeln der Kunst

thoroughly, to use every trick in the book (coll)

▶ She used every trick in the book to seduce him.

Regen • vom Regen in die Traufe kommen

to jump out of the frying pan into the fire (coll)

▶ When I switched jobs I was just jumping out of the frying pan into the fire.

Track 37

Reibach • einen Reibach machen

to make a killing (coll)

▶ He invested in copper at the right time and made a killing.

reinkriechen • jmd hinten reinkriechen
to suck up to sbd (coll), to crawl up someone's backside (vulg), to lick someone's arse (vulg)
▶ He sucked up to the boss to get his promotion and now he wants all of us to lick his arse.

riechen • Das kann ich doch nicht riechen!
How am I to know? / I'm not psychic! / I'm not clairvoyant! / I can't read your mind.

riechen • jmd nicht riechen können
not to be able to stand / bear sbd (coll), to hate sbd's guts (coll)
▶ You will never be able to get those two to work together. They can't stand each other.

Riesenwirbel • einen Riesenwirbel machen
to raise Cain
▶ They've sent the wrong papers again. I'm going down to their office to raise Cain.

Rock • bei jmd am Rockzipfel hängen
to cling to (one's) mother's apron-strings (coll)
▶ It's time he took a few risks in life – he'll never achieve anything if he always stays at home and clings to mother's apron-strings.

Rotz • Rotz und Wasser heulen
to blubber (coll), to turn on the waterworks (coll)
▶ The little boy started to blubber because his mother refused him chocolate.

ruhen • ruhe sanft
rest in peace / R.I.P.
▶ The new airport can't meet environmental needs and won't be built. R.I.P. new airport!

Ruhm • mit etwas keinen Ruhm ernten können

to win no medals for sth (coll)

▶ The judge won no medals for leniency at the end of the trial. The shortest sentence he gave any of the defendants was four years imprisonment.

Ruhm • sich in seinem Ruhm sonnen

to rest on one's laurels

▶ After winning the championship in 1986, he rested on his laurels for two years before returning to the sport.

Runden • über die Runden kommen

Gesundheit: to pull through (coll)

▶ He had a long and serious bout of influenza, but he finally pulled through.

Geld: to make (both) ends meet

▶ What with the children, the mortgage and the car, they found they were having difficulty making ends meet.

Sache • zur Sache kommen
to get down to brass tacks (coll), to get down to the nitty-gritty (coll)

Track 38

▶ The chairman of the meeting wasted no time on formalities but got down to brass tacks at once.
▶ Let's get down to the nitty gritty – who wants a pizza?

Sache • nicht bei der Sache sein
sbd's mind is elsewhere / not on sth (coll), to be woolgathering (coll), to be daydreaming
▶ I tried to explain to him about deponent verbs, but he was woolgathering and took none of it in.

Sand • jmd Sand in die Augen streuen
to pull the wool over sbd's eyes (coll)
▶ Politicians will always find a way to pull the wool over the electorate's eyes.

Sand • Sand ins Getriebe streuen
to put a spanner in the works (coll), to upset the applecart (coll)
▶ She put a spanner in the works by refusing to get the advertising department to help.

Sau • wie eine gesengte Sau
like a maniac
▶ He drove down the high street like a maniac.

sauer • sauer auf jmd sein
to have a bone to pick with sbd
▶ I have a bone to pick with my neighbour because he cut down my tree without asking me.

Schaden • den Schaden begrenzen
to cut one's losses
▶ They spent a lot of money trying to break into the Japanese market but in the end they decided to cut their losses and give up.

Schaf • das schwarze Schaf sein
to be the black sheep
▶ He's always been the black sheep of the family, wasting all his money on women and drink.

Schäfchen • sein Schäfchen ins Trockene bringen
to feather one's nest (coll)
▶ Roman tax collectors were often more concerned with feathering their own nests than with sending money back to the Imperial exchequer.

Schandtat • zu jeder Schandtat bereit sein
to be always ready for a lark (coll) / for mischief, to be game (for anything)
▶ I'm game!
▶ Sailors on shore leave are always ready for a lark.

scharf • scharf nachdenken
to think long and hard (coll)
▶ It is an interesting idea, but we shall have to think long and hard about it.

Schatz • nicht für alle Schätze der Welt
not for all the tea in China (coll)
▶ I wouldn't do your job for all the tea in China.

Track 39

Scheibe • Da kannst du dir eine Scheibe abschneiden.
you could take a leaf out of sbd's book
▶ You could take a leaf out of your brother's book and do your homework earlier – then you could watch T.V. in the evening like him.

Schema • nach Schema F vorgehen
to do sth off pat (coll), to do sth according to the book
▶ You learn something off pat.
▶ He had the music down pat and performed splendidly.

Scherflein • sein Scherflein zu etwas beitragen
to chip in (coll)
▶ I chipped in twenty pounds to the boss's retirement present.

Schlag • ein Schlag ins Wasser
a wash-out (coll), a let-down (coll), a flop (coll)
▶ We invited a rock band to come and play in the school, but they forgot half their equipment and the whole thing was a wash-out.

schlagen • Ehe ich mich schlagen lasse ...
I don't mind if I do.
▶ Would you like another cup of tea? – Yes, I don't mind if I do.

schlau • aus etwas nicht schlau werden

I can't make head or tail of it (coll), to be none the wiser for sth, it's a bit above me (coll)

▶ I can't make head or tail of this diagram. Do you understand it?

Schliche • jmd auf die Schliche kommen

to catch on to sbd (coll), to be on to (coll)

▶ The Inland Revenue are on to him. They know he is fiddling his tax return.

Schlips • sich auf den Schlips getreten fühlen

to feel put out (coll), to be miffed (coll)

▶ He's a bit miffed that you made that suggestion without consulting him beforehand.

Schnippchen • jmd ein Schnippchen schlagen

to steal a march on sbd (coll)

▶ They stole a march on us by getting their product on the market first.

Schornstein • etwas in den Schornstein schreiben können

to write sth off (coll), to ditch sth

▶ We had to write off that whole project as a dead loss.

Track 40

Schritt • den zweiten vor dem ersten Schritt tun wollen

to run before you can walk (coll)

▶ Don't try to run before you can walk.

Schuhe • jmd etwas in die Schuhe schieben

to lay the blame for sth at sbd's door, to pass the buck to sbd

▶ Don't you try to lay the blame for that at my door – I had nothing to do with it.

Schulden • mehr Schulden als Haare auf dem Kopf haben
to be up to one's ears in debt (coll)
▶ You won't get any money out of him – he's up to his ears in debt.

Schulter • etwas auf die leichte Schulter nehmen
to take sth lightly (coll), to brush sth off (coll)
▶ I heard his threat, but I didn't take it seriously – I just brushed it off.

Schulter • jmd die kalte Schulter zeigen
to give sbd the brush-off / the cold shoulder (coll), to snub sbd
▶ I pressed for a change of plan, but the management gave me the brush-off.

Schuss • ein Schuss ins Schwarze
Bull's eye (coll / exclamation), to hit the mark, to be right on (coll)
▶ That speech was right on. It got the crowd completely on our side.

schwarz • schwarz arbeiten
to moonlight
▶ I'm moonlighting as a taxi driver to put myself through law school.

schwarz • Da kannst du warten, bis du schwarz wirst!
until the cows come home
▶ You can wait there until the cows come home and never see a bus. They've changed the route.

Seele • Dann hat die liebe Seele Ruh.
That'll put an end to the matter. / That'll put us out of our misery.
MIND: "to put sbd out of the misery" can also be "to kill sbd"

Seelenruhe • in aller Seelenruhe

as cool as you please (coll), as cool as be damned (coll), as cool as a cucumber

▶ He came in here, cool as be damned, and said he had borrowed two hundred dollars from my desk.

sehen • Jeder muss sehen, wo er bleibt.

It's every man for himself.

▶ If this old boat starts to sink, it's every man for himself.

Track 41

Seiltanz • einen Seiltanz vollführen

to walk the tightrope, to do a tightrope act (coll), to do a highwire act (coll), to do a balancing act (coll)

▶ The government is doing a tightrope act, trying to keep all members of the coalition happy.

Seitensprung • einen Seitensprung machen
to have a bit on the side (coll)
▶ He has a bit on the side which his wife doesn't know about.

Semmel • weggehen wie warme Semmeln
sth sells like hot cakes (coll)
▶ All his books sell like hot cakes. He is one of the most popular authors writing today.

Senf • seinen Senf dazugeben
to shove one's oar in (coll)
▶ He's always shoving in his oar whether we've asked for his opinion or not.

sicher • so gut wie sicher
to be practically in the bag (coll)
▶ We practically have the trophy in the bag – our team is so much better than theirs.

sitzen • jmd sitzen lassen
to walk out on sbd (coll), to leave sbd
▶ His wife walked out on him after fifteen years of marriage.

Sparflamme • auf Sparflamme halten
to put sbd / sth on the back burner (coll)
▶ I have put my boyfriend on the back burner for a few weeks – he was getting too possessive.
▶ Let's put our vacation plans on the back burner until we find out what the Smiths are planning.

Spatz • Das pfeifen die Spatzen von den Dächern.
It's the talk of the town. / It's on everyone's lips.
▶ It's the talk of the town that the queen will be spending her holiday in Mecca.

Spiegel • sich etwas hinter den Spiegel stecken können
Put that in your pipe and smoke it!

Spieß • den Spieß umdrehen
to turn the tables
▶ I turned the tables on them by asking what they would have done in my place. They hadn't a clue, so they stopped criticizing.

Spitze • etwas auf die Spitze treiben
to carry sth too far (to extremes)
▶ He carried his argument too far by saying that we should not rely on our senses but upon reason alone.

Track 42

splitterfasernackt • splitterfasernackt sein
to be starkers, not to have a stitch on, to be in the raw / in one's bithday suit / in the altogether
▶ Imagine, he opened the door starkers!

springen • etwas springen lassen
to fork out for sth (coll), to stand sth (coll)
▶ I forked out for a round of drinks for the rugby team.

Sprung • den Sprung ins Ungewisse wagen
to take the plunge (coll)
▶ He hesitated a long time before he finally took the plunge and asked Amy to marry him.

Sprung • jmd auf die Sprünge helfen
to give sbd a hand (coll)
▶ I gave my son a hand with his Latin homework which he was finding difficult.

(Steck-)Nadel • eine (Steck-)Nadel im Heuhaufen suchen

to look for a needle in a hay-stack (coll)
▶ Trying to find a particular person in a city the size of Berlin is like looking for a needle in a haystack.

Stein • der Stein des Anstoßes

a cause of offence, a bone of contention
▶ The advertisements in our magazine that are aimed at children are a bone of contention to some of our readers.
MIND FF: a stumbling block: Stolperstein, Hindernis

Stein • Mir fällt ein Stein vom Herzen.

That's a load off my mind.

Sterben • kein Sterbenswörtchen

not to breathe a word (coll)
▶ Don't breathe a word to anybody – this is strictly secret.

Stern • für jmd die Sterne vom Himmel holen

to go to the ends of the earth (and back again) for sbd (coll)
▶ I would go to the ends of the earth for that girl after all she has done for me.

Stich • jmd im Stich lassen

to leave sbd in the lurch (coll), to let sbd down (coll), to leave sbd high and dry (coll), to leave sbd holding the baby (coll)
▶ They offered to help and then left us holding the baby.

stinkvornehm • stinkvornehm sein

to be a posh git (coll), to be toffee-nosed (coll), to be a toff (coll)
▶ Some posh git came along and looked at us as if we were the scum of the earth.

Track 43

Strich • nur ein Strich (in der Landschaft) sein

to be as thin as a rake/rail; to be skin and bones
▶ He is as thin as a rake – he always looks as if he could do with a square meal.

Stück • Das ist mein bestes Stück.

That is my pride and joy.
▶ Let me show you the diamond ring I inherited from my Grandma. It's my pride and joy.

Stuhl • jmd den Stuhl vor die Tür setzen

to kick sbd out (coll), to turf sbd out (coll), to boot sbd out (coll)
▶ His landlady kicked him out because he could not pay the rent.

Stunde • wissen, was die Stunde geschlagen hat

in Bezug auf das, was passiert ist: to know what's happened, to know what happened
▶ I know what happened at the meeting last Thursday.
in Bezug auf das, was passiert: to know what's cooking (coll), to know what's going on (coll)
▶ I would like to know what's cooking – lots of people are having mysterious conversations.

in Bezug auf das, was passieren wird: to know what's cooking (coll), to know which way the wind is blowing (coll)
▶ I know which way the wind is blowing as far as his job is concerned – he will have got the sack by Friday.

Sturm • gegen etwas Sturm laufen
to be up in arms against / about sth (coll)
▶ She was up in arms about how incompetently the job was being done, but nobody took any notice.

Sturm • ein Sturm im Wasserglas
a storm in a teacup (coll)
▶ I thought they had had a serious argument, but as they were clearly still good friends the next day I decided it must have been a storm in a teacup.

Süßholz • Süßholz raspeln
to whisper sweet nothings (coll)
▶ He sat in the corner of the pub, his arm round the girl, whispering sweet nothings in her ear.

Track 44

Tabula • Tabula rasa machen
to make a clean sweep (coll)
▶ We were so unimpressed with the staff working in that office that we decided to make a clean sweep and sack them all.

Tag • viel reden, wenn der Tag lang ist
to talk one's head off (coll), to talk nineteen to the dozen (coll), to talk till the cows come home
▶ The girls didn't notice. They were talking their heads off at the other end of the room.

Tasse • eine trübe Tasse sein
to be a wet blanket (coll)
▶ He is as gloomy as can be – a complete wet blanket.

Tat • jmd auf frischer Tat ertappen
to catch sbd red-handed (coll), to catch sbd in the act (of doing sth)
▶ They caught the burglars red-handed as they were breaking into the house.

Taubenschlag • Es geht hier zu wie im Taubenschlag.
It's like Piccadilly Circus here.
▶ Maggie and Andrea stopped by this morning just before Andrew left, then Sue was here for lunch and Bruce and Dolores are coming for dinner and I expect they'll stay the night. It's like Piccadilly Circus here.

Tee • Abwarten und Tee trinken.
Just wait and see.

Teller • nicht über den eigenen Tellerrand blicken können
to be unable to see beyond the end of one's nose (coll)
▶ The managers of the various shops can't see beyond the ends of their noses to the broader interests of the shopping centre as a whole.

Teufel • jmd zum Teufel jagen

to send sbd packing (coll)
▶ He came round here asking for money,
but I sent him packing.

Teufel • Wenn man vom Teufel spricht ...

Talk of the devil! / Speak of the devil!

Teufel • auf Teufel komm raus

like crazy (coll), hand over fist (coll)
▶ On holiday we spent money hand over fist.

Theater • Theater machen

**to make a big fuss about sth (coll), to make a scene about sth (coll),
to make a song and dance about sth (coll)**
▶ He made a big fuss about his flute exam, but it was quite easy really.
▶ He made a scene about our being late for dinner, but had forgotten to
make a reservation so we had to wait anyway.

Theater • jmd ein Theater vorspielen

to put on an act
▶ He seemed cheerful, I know, but he was just putting on an act for
our benefit.

Tod • jmd / etwas auf den Tod nicht ausstehen (leiden) können

to be unable to abide (stand) sbd / sth
▶ I cannot stand my geography teacher – her lessons are so boring.

Tod • über Tod und Teufel reden
to talk about everything under the sun (coll)
▶ When old friends meet after a long separation they either talk about everything under the sun or they find it hard to talk at all.

Track 45

tonangebend • tonangebend sein
to rule the roost (coll), to call the tune (coll)
▶ Grandma rules the roost in our house and nobody dares disobey her.

Toresschluss • kurz vor Toresschluss
in the nick of time (coll)
▶ I got there in the nick of time, just before the curtain went up.

Tour • krumme Touren machen
to cut corners (coll)
▶ I think he cut a few corners in his dealings with the tax man.

Tour • etwas auf die sanfte Tour versuchen
to try to get sth with a bit of soft soap (coll)
▶ He tried to get our support with a bit of soft soap, but we could see what he was up to.

Tränendrüse • auf die Tränendrüse drücken
to be a real tear-jerker (coll), four-kleenex (coll)
▶ The film "Love Story" is a real tear-jerker.

Traute • keine Traute haben
to have no guts (coll)
▶ Men have no guts. If there is dirty work to be done, you need a woman.

Treppe • die Treppe hinauffallen
to be kicked upstairs (coll)
▶ He was kicked upstairs into a position of no influence but with a fine-sounding title.

Trick • den Trick raus haben

to have got the knack of doing sth (coll)
▶ I had to practise billiards for years before I got the knack.

trocken • trocken sein

to be on the wagon
▶ Don't give him any wine, he has been on the wagon for two months now.

Tropfen • ein Tropfen auf einen heißen Stein

a drop in the ocean
▶ People tell us that all the aid that is sent from Europe and America to Africa is little more than a drop in the ocean.

Trübsal • Trübsal blasen

to be downcast, to be down in the mouth (coll), to be down in the dumps (coll)
▶ I was very down in the dumps all the time my girlfriend was away on holiday – I didn't go out once.

Tuch • wie ein rotes Tuch wirken

sth makes sbd see red (coll), to be like a red rag to a bull (coll)
▶ He is so hopelessly narrow-minded that to suggest to him that other points of view even exist is like a red rag to a bull. He sees red and loses his temper.

Tüpfelchen • das Tüpfelchen auf dem i

the icing on the cake (coll)
▶ The cream-coloured curtains are the icing on the cake.

Türke • einen Türken bauen / etwas türken

to fiddle the figures (coll)
▶ He fiddled the figures on his tax return.

Track 46

übrig • etwas für jmd / eine Sache übrig haben

to have a liking for sbd / sth, to have a soft spot (in one's heart) for sbd / sth (coll)

▶ I have had a soft spot for him all my life. I simply find him a very pleasant person.

Uhr • seine Uhr ist abgelaufen

The sands of time have run out for him. / His number's up (coll). / He's had it (coll). / His days are numbered.

Unschuld • wie die Unschuld vom Lande

to look as if butter wouldn't melt in one's mouth (coll),
to be as pure as driven snow

▶ She looks as if butter wouldn't melt in her mouth, but when she gets angry watch out!

unsterblich • unsterblich verliebt sein

to be head over heels in love

▶ He is head over heels in love with some girl from his school.

unten • ganz unten sein

to be done (coll), to be at one's wit's end

▶ I'm suffering from flu, I've just lost my job, my husband has left me ... I'm just about at my wit's end.

Track 47

verachten • Das ist nicht zu verachten!

That's not to be despised. / That's not to be scoffed at. /
That's not to be sneezed at. / It's better than a kick in the teeth.
▶ Your mother won 200 euro playing bingo? That's not to be sneezed at.

verraten • verraten und verkauft

well and truly sunk (coll), well and truly done for (coll),
sbd's goose is cooked, to be sold down the river
▶ After the Liberals withdrew their support in the House of Commons
the Government was sold down the river and could not survive.

voll • aus dem Vollen schöpfen

to make hay while the sun shines
▶ After the government agreed to support the project the managers found
themselves able to make hay while the sun shone.
▶ Mum isn't home. Let's make hay while the sun shines and bake some
cookies!

Vordermann • auf Vordermann bringen

jmd: to get sbd to shape up (coll), to get sbd / sth into shape
▶ The lieutenant told the sergeant he would have to get his men to shape
up if they were to be ready to go into battle by May 1st.
etwas: to get sth ship-shape and Bristol-fashion (coll)
▶ I gave the schoolgirls twenty minutes to clear up the mess they had made
and get the place ship-shape and Bristol-fashion again.
Kenntnisse: to brush sth up (coll)
▶ I wanted to brush up my Italian before I went to visit my friend in Rome.

vormachen • sich nichts vormachen lassen

to be nobody's fool (coll)
▶ He's nobody's fool and sees quite clearly what the situation is.

Track 48

Wahl • keine Wahl haben
Hobson's choice
▶ We have Hobson's choice – damned if we do, and damned if we don't.

wahnsinnig • Das kann einen ja wahnsinnig machen!
enough to drive you to drink
▶ His heavy metal music is enough to drive me to drink!

wahr • so wahr ich hier stehe
as sure as eggs is eggs (coll), as sure as I am standing here
▶ If I lend you the book, you'll forget to bring it back, as sure as eggs is eggs.

Wahrheit • Sie nimmt es mit der Wahrheit nicht so genau.
You have to take what she says with a pinch of salt.

Wand • die Wand hochgehen (vor Wut)
to hit the roof, to blow one's top, to go up the wall (coll)
▶ He went right up the wall when he heard about how stupidly we had behaved.

warm • sich jmd warm halten

to keep in with sbd (coll)
▶ I am very keen on keeping in with the boss, now that the possibility of promotion has come up.

warm • mit jmd (nicht) warm werden können

to be not sbd's type, we don't really hit it off
▶ We've worked together in the same office for years, but we don't really hit it off.

Wasser • mit allen Wassern gewaschen sein

to know all the tricks in the book (coll)
▶ That lawyer is extremely experienced and he knows all the tricks in the book.

Wecker • jmd auf den Wecker gehen (fallen)

to get on sbd's nerves (coll), to get on sbd's wick (coll),
to drive sbd up the wall (coll)
▶ My new secretary chews gum all the time, which really gets on my nerves.

Weg • Der gerade Weg ist der kürzeste.

Honesty is the best policy.

Weg • sich selbst im Wege stehen

to be one's own worst enemy (coll)
▶ He is perfectly intelligent, but he is his own worst enemy. He simply cannot discipline himself to give up some of his pleasures and get down to work.

Weg • jmd nicht über den Weg trauen
not to trust sbd an inch (coll), not to trust sbd as far as one can throw them (coll), not to trust sbd across the street (coll), not to trust sbd out of one's sight (coll)
▶ The head of my school seems pleasant enough, but I don't trust her an inch. She has tricked me too often.

Weihnachtsgans • jmd ausnehmen wie eine Weihnachtsgans
to fleece sbd (coll), to take sbd to the cleaners (coll)
▶ The greedy young girl fleeced her wealthy boyfriend for as much as she could get and then left him.

Wein • jmd reinen Wein einschenken
to tell sbd the truth, to come clean with sbd (coll), to talk turkey (A.E.)
▶ After prevaricating for a few minutes he told the boss the truth – that he had lost the vital papers.
▶ Let's talk turkey. Have you lost those important papers? Yes or no?

Wein • heimlich Wein trinken und öffentlich Wasser predigen
not to practise what one preaches
▶ He liked his subordinates to have tidy desks, but he did not practise what he preached and never bothered to tidy his own.
▶ Practise what you preach and tidy your desk!

Track 49

Wellen • hohe Wellen schlagen
to create a stir (coll)
▶ He created quite a stir among the political journalists with his announcement that he intended to challenge the Prime Minister for the party leadership.

Weste • eine weiße Weste haben
to have a clean slate (coll)
▶ He has never been in trouble with the police and has a clean slate.

Westentasche • etwas wie seine Westentasche kennen
to know sth like the back of one's hand (coll)
▶ I know Paris like the back of my hand, having lived there for several years when I was young.

Wiesel • (flink) wie ein Wiesel
as quick as a flash (coll)
▶ Quick as a flash he ran to the wicket, raised his hand and caught the ball.

Wind • in den Wind schlagen
guten Rat: to turn a deaf ear to sth
▶ He turned a deaf ear to my advice and continued to make the same mistakes over and over again.
Vorsicht, Vernunft: to throw / cast sth to the winds (coll)
▶ He threw caution to the winds and decided to invest all his money in a risky speculation.

windelweich • jmd windelweich schlagen
to beat the living daylights out of sbd (coll)
▶ The thugs beat the living daylights out of the two policemen.

Wolf • mit den Wölfen heulen
to go with the crowd (coll), to swim with the tide
▶ Youngsters often don't think for themselves – they simply go with the crowd.

Wolke • aus allen Wolken fallen
to be gobsmacked (by sth) (coll), to be bowled over (coll)
▶ The teacher listened to the entire discussion and was bowled over by the amount the youngsters knew.

Wolle • sich mit jmd in die Wolle kriegen

to fall out with sbd (coll), to have a row with sbd (coll)

▶ I had a row with him about the new computer system he said we needed. I thought it would be a waste of money.

Wort • jmd beim Wort nehmen

to take sbd up on an offer (coll)

▶ He said he would drive me home in his car and I took him up on his offer.

Wort • jmd mit leeren Worten abspeisen

to leave sbd empty handed

▶ He expected to gain from the negotiations, but was left empty handed.

Track 50

X-mal

umpteen times (coll)

▶ I have explained it to you umpteen times!

Track 51

Zahn • jmd den Zahn ziehen

to scotch that (coll), to put paid to that (coll), to put the (tin) lid on that (coll), to knock that on the head (coll)

▶ My daughter really wanted to go to Spain on holiday, but I had to scotch that.

Zahn • die Zähne zusammenbeißen

to bite on the bullet, to grit one's teeth and keep going, to keep a stiff upper lip (coll)

▶ He was very upset when his girlfriend left him, but he kept a stiff upper lip and did not show his feelings.

Zeche • die Zeche bezahlen müssen

bezahlen: to foot the bill (coll)

▶ I had to foot the bill for the repairs to my son's car.

Verantwortung übernehmen: to take the rap (coll), to face the music (coll), to carry the can (coll), to be left holding the baby (coll)

▶ He had to take the rap for making a mess of the new accounting system.

Zeit • Spare in der Zeit, so hast du in der Not. (prov)

to put sth by, to save (for a rainy day)

▶ You should always save for a rainy day.

zeitlich • das Zeitliche segnen

to go the way of all flesh (coll)

▶ Our rowing club has been losing members for years, and now it has gone the way of all flesh.

Zepter • das Zepter schwingen

to call the tune (coll), to rule the roost (coll), to lay down the law (coll)

▶ The boss's son calls the tune around here – no-one else has any influence at all.

Zeter • Zeter und Mordio schreien

to scream blue/bloody murder (coll), to raise a hue and cry (coll), to raise Cain (coll), to scream the place down (coll), to raise merry hell (coll)

▶ As soon as they heard about the cuts that were to be made in their department all the sociologists screamed blue murder and protested to the Treasurer of the university.

Zeug • was das Zeug hält

Track 52

like mad (coll), for all one is worth (coll), like anything (coll), like blazes (coll), hell for leather (coll), like a bat out of hell (coll)

▶ The tennis player chased after the ball like mad, but could not reach it before it bounced.

Zubrot

to earn (make) a bit on the side (coll)

▶ He has earned a bit on the side with his articles for newspapers.

Zuckerbrot • mit Zuckerbrot und Peitsche

with the carrot and stick treatment

▶ The only way to teach some children is with the carrot and stick treatment, they say.

Zug • in den letzten Zügen liegen

bald sterben: to be on one's last legs (coll), to be at the end of one's days, to be approaching the end of one's days, to be at death's door, to have one foot in the grave (coll)

▶ My dog is very old and on his last legs. I ought to have him put down.

mit etwas fast fertig sein: to be on the last lap (coll), to be in the home stretch (coll)

▶ We are in the home stretch and will have it finished by next week.

Zweifel • über jeden Zweifel erhaben sein

to be as honest as the day is long
▶ He won't overcharge you. He is as honest as the day is long.

Zwickmühle • in einer Zwickmühle sein

it's catch 22 (coll), to be damned if one does and damned
if one doesn't (coll), to be in a dilemma, to be caught between
two stools
▶ There is no right thing to do. Anything we do will be wrong. –
It's catch 22.

Register

Register

from start to finish   6
frost   23
Fuck off!   62
full monty   21
full of beans   65

G
get a good hiding   6
get a good thrashing   6
get down to brass tacks   71
get down to the nitty-gritty   71
get fresh   45
get hot under the collar   67
get in sbd's way   28
get into hot water   56
get off lightly   11
get off with   8
get on sbd's nerves   89
get on sbd's wick   89
get one's fingers burnt   56
get out of bed on the wrong side   14
get out of sth   8
get sbd/sth into shape   87
get sth off one's chest   53
get sth on the black market   33
get sth ship-shape and Bristol-fashion   87
get sth through channels   33
get sth under the counter   33
get things back on the rails   42
get/knuckle down to sth   34
give a ball-park figure   19
give oneself airs   63
give sbd a bollocking   47
give sbd a dressing-down   47
give sbd a hand   78
give sbd a rocket   47
give sbd a wide berth   16
give sbd an earful   47
give sbd hell   39
give sbd the brush-off   75
give sbd the cold shoulder   75
give sbd three cheers   38
give somebody a lecture   47
give sth the finishing touch   65
give the game away   43
give up the ghost   28

give vent to one's feelings   54
give/budge an inch   36
go/be sent from pillar post   65
go down the drain   15
go down the pan   15
go down the tubes   15
go downhill   15
go Dutch   43
go off the rails   67
go over the top   10
go phut   15
go the way of all flesh   93
go through the roof   19
go to pot   15
go to the dogs   15, 67
go to the ends of the earth (and back again) for sbd   79
go up the wall   88
go West   41
go with the crowd   91
go/be down the drain   23
gobsmacked   91
Good grief!   42
good/real sport   64
gossip   45
great bloke   64
great guy   64
green with envy   58
grin and bear it   56
grin from ear to ear   39
grin like a Cheshire cat   39
grit one's teeth and keep going   93

H
hair-raising   32
hand in glove with sbd   19
hand over fist   83
handle sb with kid gloves   23
hanging by a thread   45
hatch a plot   67
hate sbd's guts   63, 69
haul sbd over the coals   28
have a bit on the side   77
have a bone to pick with sbd   40, 71
have a clean slate   91
have a clue   22
have a finger in the pie   33
have a kip   60

have a liking for   86
have a lot on one's plate   61
have a row with sbd   92
have a say in the business   33
have a screw loose   19
have a skeleton in the cupboard   50
have a snooze   60
have a soft spot (in one's heart) for   86
have a sweet tooth   50
have a touch of   13
have ants in your pants   66
have fallen out   51
have forty winks   60
have got one's eye on sbd   44
have got the hang/knack of sth   46, 85
have had a few   8
have had it   23
have money to burn   29
have no flies on one   46
have no guts   84
have one foot in the grave   94
have ruin stare one in the face   58
have sbd on   10
have sbd up on one's carpet   47
have sbd/sth on one's hands   33
have sth first hand   33
have sth hot off the press   33
have sth straight from source   33
have sth straight from the horse's mouth   33
have sth up one's sleeve   38
have sticky fingers   26
have the faintest (idea)   22
have the fidgets   66
have the foggiest (idea)   22
have to bite the bullet   9
have/get Delhi belly   61
have/get dog-ears   24
have/get gippy tummy   61
have/get the runs   61
have/get the trots   61
have/take a nap   60
hazard a rough guess at   19

Register

Register